Clare Songbirds Publishing House Poetry Series
ISBN 978-1-947653-85-6
Clare Songbirds Publishing House
Give Water to the Potter © 2020 KR Staller

All Rights Reserved. Permission to reprint individual poems must be obtained from the author who owns the copyright.

Printed in the United States of America
FIRST EDITION

Clare Songbirds Publishing House Mission Statement:
Clare Songbirds Publishing House was established to provide a print forum for the creation of limited edition, fine art from poets and writers, both established and emerging. We strive to reignite and continue a tradition of quality, accessible literary arts to the national and international community of writers, and readers. Chapbook manuscripts are carefully chosen for their ability to propel the expansion of art and ideas in literary form. We provide an accessible way to promote the art of words in order to resonate with, and impact, readers not yet familiar with the siren song of poets and writers. Clare Songbirds Publishing House espouses a singular cultural development where poetry creates community and becomes commonplace in public places.

140 Cottage Street
Auburn, New York 13021
www.claresongbirdspub.com

Contents

Hard Slab
7

Paper
8

Teapot
9

Pencil
10

Brush Spawn
11

My Dad Wanted to Know Why I Wasn't a Christian
12

Pigment
13

Broken Pots
14

Turp
15

Waterlogged Colored Pencil
17

Throwing Rocks
18

The author wishes to thank the following publications for originally publishing the works in the book.

"Brush Spawn" winner of the 2018 *Lewis Turco Formal Poetry Award.*

"Throwing Rocks" *We Are Lake Ontario* chapbook and exhibit, 2018

To the artists who spend all night in the studio, to the creatives who question their purposes, and above all, to Laura Donnelly, the true reason I am a poet to this day.

Hard Slab

This isn't about following
a routine of sitting in church and having the wafting
perfume of that old lady clog your
senses and lull you

in that trap. Rather
the opposite, when the bull
storms down the atheist walls and shatters
the teapots. It's unexpectedly

anticipated, following the white
van home. That stubborn bull
who wouldn't lie

down

for that knife of a Sunday
because Friday was spent
carving templates and throwing

clay against the table, unharmed
except for the crack and the
whitened edges.
Hard slabbed marked with orange

underglaze but the leather remains
stubbornly hard and unwilling
to accept the scored marks
and flaked coils.

Paper

the pagan dipped the mahogany wand
into cauldron of milk

swirling the net.
ritual dance for the gods

of old, scolding reserved
for child cross road without

looking twice.
the pagan's neck agitated,

divorced flour, fingerprinted. wood
roll out spells

on old cotton, capturing cryptic
symbols, whisks water away

Teapot

snow drifts off the roof as dust.
street light catching each particle to cast a flame
until there is a diminutive fire outside my window.

before the clay can form the pot
it must be coaxed into the overstuffed pillow ball
and snout elongated to silhouette the spout.

wagon wheels on shelves, horse hooves
in the barn, the option is limited
with the porous styrofoam particles rising from old castings.

leak the brown slit from the cut open,
roast the quabby terracotta by stoking the flames beyond my window,
shave down the seams with the wooden blade,

glass paint sear flowers on edges with a steady hand,
the same hand held to my neck as I bid you adieu.
china before me stale with your promise.

pot dangled in glaze,
uprooted and chilled,
as the teapot tips and lets excess drain from the openings.

Photo by Tafilah Yusof from Pixabay

Pencil

Clouds shimmer over the desktop moon
        haze shutters play peekaboo
           with a dreaming infant. Pencil, specifically
the number 2, clutched in hand

where baby fat puddles from carbon

bones. A vase scribbled on the sketch pad,
    ceramic masterpiece where the irony
      of the clay in your graphite tip
leaks down the industrial paper

Brush Spawn

Icebergs float on the lake, imperfections
where artist had a lapse of acumen.
On her brush white paint lingered, black sections
contrasted by silver strips. The hairs bloom in

                            unison together, clipped and have been
                      glued to wood. Compressed so nothing would fall
                          free, the icebergs don't last long on the gin
                              candy waters. Leaf falls, path sure by scrawl

in wind, lightning upon the silent bawl
canvas. Water tumbles from the painting,
icecaps gaining depth, consuming the doll
on her painting stool. Sun slowly raining,

                                    she waits for the drying gesso under
                                  bristles so she might amend her blunder.

My Dad Wanted to Know Why I Wasn't Christian

The proclaimed son
became tipsy on glasses of water.
His father couldn't guess why, but the boy made
each sip an alcoholic twang.
In a drunken, slobbering state
he looked for those who held their beliefs
in the deeds of other beings. A supernatural predicament.
Chuckling and stumbling,

waving his hand and shaking his head,
he transformed my working clay
from the dark plasticity
into the leather hide of the stubborn bull
who refused to be sacrificed on Sundays.
Beaten, bloodied, broken.
Torrent of wind cooled the rageous hide,
clay thickening, wooden tool
useless against works of
drunken fools.

Pigment
Based on the children's rhyme, "There's a Hole in My Bucket"

Why do you have a bottle of arsenic?
    Because it mixes with thiosulfate.
What's that?
    A solution of sulfate and oxygen.
Why do you need the science equipment?
    Combined they produce this pigment, here.
What do you need that?
    To mix it with oil.
Why do you mix it with oil?
    I'm creating Tuscan yellow.
What do you need that yellow for?
    The tired trees on this drought ridden field need it.
Why is there a drought?
    There isn't enough rain.
Where is the rain?
    Away so my paint can dry.

Broken Pots

Street light catching each particle to cast a flame
to shadow an elephant creeping in dusk,

snout elongated to silhouette the calfs
that lie dead in the stream bare

of water for millennium.
Porous styrofoam particles rise from old carbon

bone dry. The indigenous place the outlines
of the water pot, roasting the quabby terracotta

by flattery flames. Crackling and popping, the bones
cascade into the graves of those decomposing elephants.

Turp

Queen, Queen Caroline,
Washed her hair in turpentine,
Turpentine made it shine,
Queen, Queen Caroline.
~Nursery Rhyme

Americans waged a war on terebinth trees
before they could claim the golden drizzle.
Honey rosin remains a byproduct of the process,
resinous sap once the goal to brighten colors
now is used as thinner. Corroded cans

      squat on the splotted desk, risque spontaneous
      combustion lingers alongside the tart whiff
      of turpentine. Shiver within metal
      bastille to ameliorate coruscating red

and blue streaks. Turp attenuating the oil coats
depicting the rain stick filled with paxil
and the fisher cat huffing and puffing, portrayed on the painting.
Tail flaccid as he lays to rest his quest,
cracked hands one with the baroque canvas.

Waterlogged Colored Pencil

Reduce the wax, Momma said, we ain't burning candles tonight.

We flourishing in that lake outside the window, hop on one foot burnishing those pink flamingo just to show Momma that look, look I know the meaning of balance. I derive directly from that extrusion machine after I've been compressed from these crumbs. My pigment was enough to make batches that cedar would call out, here. Here is the length of that pencil for that artist there. There. There that artist. How that artist draws. I call enough for the wood, strapped as I am with glue to the engraving carved with just enough space for me, just enough space for cedar to enclose me with a musky embrace. Despite my efforts, Momma sighs when my sharpened end pricks her finger, I didn't pass her quality test of that one hundred metres of writing but Momma can't you see, you see, you took the paper from my burning embered tip, stole the smoke from my lungs, extinguished my tobacco with the wax you scorned, the wax along my label that claims I'm from your womb, I originate from the witches cathedral of towering iron and adhesion, submerged and impregnated in the chemical vat as you wanted me to paint you a picture of my reflection on the rocks. I was solid before you knew how to deluge me to fit your brush stroke. Momma you dipped varnish on one end so my exterior can match your assumptions that weighs my ingredients.

We ain't burning candles tonight, Momma said. We ain't burning, we just lost in the night.

Throwing Rocks

I.

I let you climb inside of me. I let you slide
down to me. I let you burn the rocks

and watch them pop. They call me great
because my depth is further than my brother, they call me great

as I kept Huron from Iroquois. Great,
because I've seen human settlers on my border, I've seen the fox

win the fish, I've seen the student row
to my center with a rack of liquor. Ain't it

great? And when you come to me and watch my white
foam tap the shoulder of the rocks you've the gall

to enter me. What did you expect me to do, but to leave kisses
over your stomach, my black tinting your blue. I could have written

you a hundred love poems, I could have let you lose
your way in the rolling fog. I left you the sturgeon

and salmon but it wasn't enough. You
kept coming back in your overalls and wading

onto my shores. Commercialization and phosphates
clog my sinuses as your dalliances leave lamprey,

rock me to my
knees, once great.

II.

Let me pause as I
give water to the potter. He said

Jesus was a potter, but you're not some messiah walking this land
you had stolen from my kindred. I give water to the

potter, who remains crouched before their wheel, a prayer in the form of mud
hands. You tried to make paint from my shells, the gulls

brought you the clams. I give water
to the potter, and the potter didn't bother to come and give

the thanks to me. As you leave the carcass, you don't need
to be bothered because I'm not breathing, I'm just pushing

waves and cradling the sun to sleep. I give
water to the potter who uses my sun to mold an idea

onto the wheel. I give water to the potter but the potter never
asked for my silt, never asked for my ecosystem.

III.

I give water
to the.

Stop. I give
water to. No. I give

water. Not
yet. I give.

I
give

IV.

The potter watched the wheel
turn and turn as the sun spun and spun

around me. Connecting two lands of vast
misunderstanding, kindness is not my forte

as you skim rocks over my surface. You think it's a game
to see how many times you can

puncture my skin, how many times you can watch
me touch the sky for solidarity, you think it's a game

as I seep to my darkest depth
and move these rocks you've placed in me.

K. R. Staller is an advocate for the arts, animal lover, and alumni of State University of New York at Oswego. Staller can be found in Eastern Connecticut, performing spoken word pieces and creating fine art.

www.ingramcontent.com/pod-product-compliance
Lightning Source LLC
Chambersburg PA
CBHW052130110526
44592CB00013B/1829